How to Make Dating Not Suck

To the shitty exes who inspired several pages in this book: I can laugh about it now. Hope you're full of regret and I cross your mind on a weekly basis.

xoxo

Carina Maggar

How to Make Dating Not Suck

Laurence King

Slot Machines and Broken Dreams

The word "date" originates from the medieval Latin "to dare". Pretty appropriate if you ask me. It takes courage and guts to voluntarily chuck yourself into the dating ring. Why? Because modern dating is a shitshow. But you must know that already, or you wouldn't be holding this book.

An estimated 192,857 dates occur in London alone each day. Overwhelming choice, superficial interactions, unrealistic expectations, "hook-up" culture and inconsistent communication all lead to social fatigue and early-onset arthritis in our thumbs. Sometimes online dating can feel like a job; it's time-consuming and draining having the same conversations multiple times a day, often simultaneously. There are only so many inventive/hilarious/engaging ways to answer "Hey, what you up to?" before wanting to lob your phone into a hedge.

A swipe based on a few pixels has made the process transactional, and because of that, we've become increasingly judgemental yet disposable. "They look too short", "their jeans are too tight" or "they spelt that word wrong in their bio" have all become reasonable justifications as to why someone might not be to our liking and it's made us fickle. Designed like slot machines in a casino, dating apps have literally rewired our brains. Technology has changed how we communicate and our exchanges have become baseless.

I've had my fair share of rubbish dates leading up to getting where I am today. Returning home and collapsing on the bed after one too many gin and tonics thinking that was a total waste of my time, money and energy. Dates are nerve-wracking and tiring. I used to hate the pressure of bringing my best-self; funny but not too funny, confident but never cocky, just the right balance of reserved meets complete over-sharer. Asking the right questions, being prepared with the right answers.

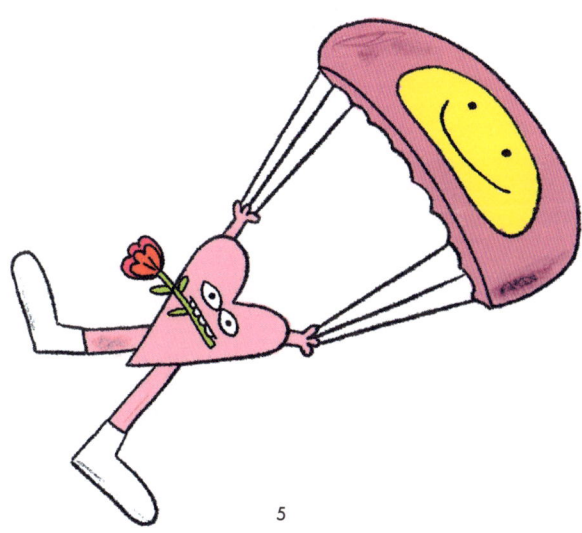

The anxiety of filling long silences. What if they don't think I look like my photos? What if they don't get my humour? What if we run out of things to talk about? What if I want to escape within 20 seconds of meeting them? The dread of arriving at the location knowing the other person was already there and having to speedily scan the room for their face. Don't even get me started on stressing over what to wear or how to appropriately end the evening.

Finding a partner today is harder than it was 20 years ago — fact. Online dating equals indecision and dissatisfaction. Have you ever walked into a shop and got so overwhelmed that you've immediately made a U-turn and walked out? As a numbers game, the more dates you go on, the more likely you are to find someone. But is that really the case? Give yourself time. Get to the bottom of the values you're searching for in a partner. "Tall, dark and handsome" isn't enough. The movies lie to us. The songs lie to us. Past generations also lie to us.

There's also so much for us to balance these days and it's impossible to nail them all; careers, self-care, social lives and all the demands that come along with each of them. Having said that, marriage and monogamy are no longer so appealing; for many of us, finding a life partner is not the ultimate goal.

For balance (and because of experience) the second half of this book covers all things heartbreak; another topic I feel pretty well seasoned in. Not wanting to get out of bed, losing your appetite, crying in the shower, wandering aimlessly around cemeteries (not joking). Best believe, I've been there and it took a long time to pick myself up again. Now a blessing, but at the time I wanted nothing more than the ground to swallow me up.

It was only fair I delved into both ends of the spectrum: looking for love and trying to get over it. I'm not sure which side I'd rather be on. For anyone actively on the dating scene right now, my thoughts and prayers are with you during this difficult time.

Love Can Happen in the Strangest of Places

Putting petrol in your car, in line at the supermarket, ordering popcorn at the cinema. You just have to be open enough to spot it and act on it. If they're taken or not interested, who cares? Be like Kobe and shoot your shot.

A few years ago, I was on a bus minding my own business when a woman got on, taking the spare seat next to a guy. They were making small talk and giggling for the entirety of the journey. When it got to his stop he asked for her number, or if she happened to be free for a coffee. They got off the bus together as if they'd known each other for years. They're probably married now.

"Hope You Brought an Umbrella"

Talk of heatwaves, tropical droughts or torrential rain is off the menu. Instead, ask them their plans for the following day, what kind of music they listen to, or their final prison meal. If all else fails, a game of Would You Rather is a great choice.

At first, the date might feel awkward – like the silence is lasting an eternity – but most likely it's not, and it's in your head. The purpose of going on a date is to get to know the person, so ask questions you'd genuinely like to know the answers to.

If you're struggling to think of conversation starters, fret not, get a trusty AI pal to do it for you. Take notes and come prepared.

Some Things That Really Matter

Flirting isn't about twirling your hair and licking your lips. Stop trying to seduce them superficially. Let go of all the surface stuff and really get to know the person on a deeper level. Connecting emotionally and intellectually is the real turn on. Think about:

- Body language
- Eye contact
- Manners*
- Facial expressions
- How you treat the staff
- How much you talk about yourself
- What you're wearing
- What you smell like
- Hygiene

*Keep your elbows off the table, as well as politics. A 2024 survey showed that people are more attracted to their date when they find out they're registered to vote (and way less attractive when they discover you don't share the same views, so keep schtum for now).

What Even Am I?

People are realising more and more that they might not be the heterosexual person they once thought they were. Maybe you're considering joining the other team. Well, now's the time to take the plunge. No, you're not having an existential crisis. You're exploring your horizons and expanding your dating pool.

My Milkshake Brings All the (Fuck) Boys (and Girls) to the Yard

Are you attracting the same kind of people constantly? Do your dates feel uninspiring? It's probably because you've reached burnout and you're fed up. Too many dates with the wrong mentality and attitude will lead to you asking questions like, "What's wrong with me?" or "Why did my friends find it so easy to meet someone?" It could also be that you're emotionally drained and not setting the right boundaries. Take some time away from serial dating to re-evaluate exactly what it is you're looking for in a partner, and don't make exceptions out of desperation. It's a Ferris wheel of fickle people out there. Going on three dates every week is not what will lead to the right relationship.

Monogamy Is Dead

On the other hand, the idea that we must spend our entire life with one person is wild. Societal pressures have shifted; we're realising that it's very unrealistic. People change, circumstances change, life moves at a fast pace and our wants, needs and desires evolve alongside that.

Romantic films and novels have fooled us into thinking this kind of eternal love is attainable, but the truth is it's the case for very few.

P.S. Nearly all male characters in romcoms and movies were created by women. I highly doubt you'll find many Ryan Goslings willing to build your dream white house with blue shutters and a room overlooking the river knocking about your local.

Balloons at the Bus Stop

"It was our first and only date. I texted her the next day to say that we'd be better off as friends. She told me I'd made the biggest mistake of my life, that I'd live to regret it and she "wouldn't give up on us". Two months later she was waiting for me at the bus stop outside my house with some chocolates and a balloon that said "Sorry". Long story short, I now have a restraining order in place."

Cool, Calm and Exfoliated

You might hate small talk or just find the idea of going on a first date completely nerve-wracking, and that's OK. My advice would be to do whatever you need to get comfortable before your date. Maybe it's taking a long shower, trimming or shaving, exfoliating, setting intentions, meditating, moisturizing from head to toe, putting your lucky pants on, sipping a cocktail (or tea), taking some deep breaths in the mirror, having a little singalong and avoiding any food that will make you bloated. If you're feeling especially uncomfortable in your own skin, practising self-compassion is the first step.

A 2014 study by Stanford found that self-compassion reduces cortisol and increases resilience. So, when you're on a date and silently panicking, that's your body going into fight or flight mode, meaning your resilience is low and your cortisol is high. Breathe in, freak out. Allow yourself to feel it all and remember that they're on a date with you because they want to be.

"Why Are You Still Single?"

Oh, I don't know, maybe because I'm emotionally unstable and unavailable and have no idea what I want in life? Or maybe I'm too needy, or not needy enough? It could be my unresolved childhood trauma? Daddy issues? Maybe I'm just literally no one's cup of tea.

Find Me a Find, Catch Me a Catch

- A dating app for people who love people in uniform
- A dating app for people who love bacon
- A dating app for men with beards
- A dating app for people who love salad
- A dating app for people with grey hair
- A dating app for the gluten-intolerant (or those who don't eat bread)
- A dating app for tall people
- A dating app for short people
- A dating app for mullet lovers
- A dating app for married people
- A dating app for people with STIs
- A dating app for people on the same flight
- A dating app for farmers
- A dating app for ugly people
- A dating app for people with dogs
- A dating app for people who hate dating apps

All of the above really exist. Yes, all of them. As if all bases weren't already covered, Japan's fertility rate recently dropped to the lowest it's ever been, resulting in the government launching a dating app designed to encourage baby-making. How romantic.

Ick Happens

They might be wearing a fragrance that makes you heave, perhaps they've loosely draped a sweater over their shoulders, or maybe their jeans are so tight you can see the outline of their kneecaps. Whatever the reason, whatever the ick, put the judgemental thoughts aside and try to see them for who they are as a person.

The Bare Minimum

The other person is putting time and effort into this, the least you can do is the same. Shower before your date. Make sure you're not putting on damp clothes (the worst smell in the world). This is the very bare minimum. If you'd like to do more than the bare minimum, might I suggest the following:

- Brush your teeth (and stash some gum in your pocket)
- Clean the dirt out your nails and trim them
- Add a spritz of perfume
- Iron your shirt if you're wearing one
- Don't forget deodorant

Triangles and Tribulations

"I met him at a bar; he approached me in line for a drink. He was in his late twenties, very handsome, dressed in a three-piece suit. He smelt expensive.

I gave him my number and was excited to hear from him. A few days later he invited me over for a "homecooked meal". I got my hair and nails done and spent hours choosing the perfect outfit. When I arrived, he opened the door in a T-shirt and boxers with toy robots on them. He offered me some tap water and we sat on the floor of his bedroom at his parents' house eating microwave popcorn and cheese sandwiches cut into triangles. About an hour in, when he suggested we watch back-to-back episodes of *Power Rangers*, I pretended to get an emergency call from a friend and was out of there within minutes. He was completely different to the guy I met the week before."

Tidy Your Room

Before you leave for your date make your bed, change your sheets and get rid of scrunchy tissues and stiff hand towels. Give your kitchen a quick clean and remove the dirty dishes from the sink and the mouldy veg in the fridge. You don't know if you might be accompanied by a guest on your return. The same goes for your bathroom: remove all traces of skid marks and curly pubes.

Feeling Delulu?

It's been said that rejection is protection, meaning if you're having to work hard in your pursuit of someone – whether that's chasing responses to texts, or feeling like you're doing all of the organizing and planning of dates – it just might be that this is the universe warning you that it's not meant to be. It should never feel like you're being annoying or persistent, or having to convince someone you're worth their time or attention.

Sidenote: Friends are known to encourage delulu. Of course they mean well, they're trying to protect your feelings. They'll offer all sorts of crazy explanations as to why you haven't heard from them; they've definitely lost their phone/been hit by a bus/got their head stuck in the fridge/are stranded on a desert island with no signal/ have been sent on a mission to outer space in search of alien life. It's best to keep a straight-talking, no-bullshit friend on the sidelines who will tell it like it is.

Lower Those Expectations...

Don't set the bar so high that it's unrealistic. Someone who is emotionally available; is emotionally intelligent; is actually intelligent; has a good job; earns good money; dresses well; dances well; smells good; has all their teeth; has a good amount of hair; is of reasonable height; and is mentally stable is about as unlikely as encountering a vaquita* mid-snorkel.

* The vaquita is the most endangered marine mammal in the world. Total population = 10.

Or Up Your Standards

Don't set the bar so low that you're impressed by the most basic of things, such as they: walked you to your bus stop; texted you back within a reasonable time; texted you back at all; got you a card on your birthday; paid you a compliment; didn't cancel the date; were on time; didn't pressure you for anything physical on the first date; washed before they left the house; got your name right.

I'll Show You Mine if You Show Me Yours

I'm not saying don't send nudes, but before you press send, be very aware that those photos will indefinitely be in someone else's possession. Would it bother you to know they're still zooming in on your bits in ten years' time when you no longer speak?

Kate Bush

Keep running up that hill. The more terrible dates you have, the closer you'll be to knowing what you're looking for. Dating teaches you a lot about yourself, like: is their career as important as you thought? Do you really care if they live with their parents? Is height really a non-negotiable? If you tune in to your critical thoughts and inner commentary when it comes to judging other people's lives, you might start questioning your own character and prejudices for the better.

Pressure, Pickiness and Protecting Yourself from the Patriarchy

Lily Womble is sparking a feminist revolution in the way we date and find love. Originally a matchmaker, now a dating coach, her company Date Brazen has helped hundreds of women create love lives that are joyful-as-hell.

I chatted to her about asking yourself deeper questions, the vulnerability involved in dating and the danger in knowing what you want.

Apps Have Gamified Dating Culture

"Dating has always been a microcosm of our well-being. It's every hope, joy, dream, fear, insecurity and desire that we have as humans. It's an incredibly vulnerable act. And then you throw in patriarchal conditioning and other forms of oppression that make our lives feel terrible, and what you get is a hot soup of a culture that makes single women specifically feel behind. There's an inherent pressure to perform in your dating life. If you're in your thirties and successful but you're not coupled up, there's this sense that other people have succeeded. You may start to think "What's wrong with me?", and it's only exacerbated by dating app marketing messages that tell users that it should be easy – all it takes is one swipe. Dating apps have gamified our dating culture. Our use of them with their intended design of a slot machine has made people feel like a number, which reduces individuality and makes people feel trapped."

Over-functioning, Under-functioning

"There are two responses to the stimuli of dating: over-functioning and under-functioning. Both are a form of self-protection that either protects you from settling and being with the wrong person, or protects you from rejection. Over-functioning is rigidity, such as looking for somebody six feet tall, who went to an Ivy League school, who is thirty-four and has never been married. Under-functioning is looking for somebody "nice" with a job. It needs to go deeper. Pickiness is knowing what you want, but rigidity is trying to protect yourself in a harmful way.

If my client says, "I want somebody intelligent," we ask deeper questions and they usually realize what they actually want is somebody "joyfully nerdy", and then we work on their bespoke definition of that. These are called "essence-based preferences". Think more vividly; it'll make it easier to set boundaries with the wrong people and allows you to ask the right questions."

The Fiery Hellscape
of the Patriarchy

"'You're too picky' is a phrase born of the
patriarchy. As one example of this, in the US,
it wasn't until 50 years ago that a woman could
have a credit card without her husband's
permission. Back then, you'd have to settle
romantically in order to thrive economically.
Wanting what you want now disrupts the
status quo of agency and choice. If we look
at the declining birth rate, the government
(in the US at least) is incentivizing people
to have babies, and to settle quickly and be
less picky. That's just one reason why there's
such pressure for women to marry."

Lily's advice book, *Thank You, More Please: A Feminist
Guide to Breaking Dumb Dating Rules and Finding Love*,
is available everywhere books are sold.

I Don't Recommend the "Guess What Age I Am?" Game

Guess too young and it might come off as fake and predictable. Guess too old and it's insulting. Guess just right and they might have expected a different answer. You can't win, and no one's going to be honest anyway.

"You look so good for your age!" is one of those insults disguised as a compliment. Avoid at all costs.

Dora the Explorer

This is a polite suggestion to clear your search history. If you've been Googling someone (such as the person you're on a date with) or something embarrassing, it's wise to clear your search history or close those tabs before going on your date. What if they ask to borrow your phone? What if they come back to yours, want to use your TV or laptop, and you've just searched "How to make someone fall in love with me?", "How to bleach my asshole?" or even worse, their LinkedIn profile. Beware. Cringey things can happen when your device is in someone else's hands, and you might not recover.

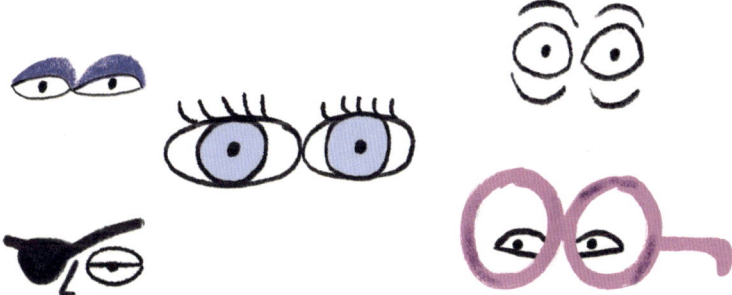

Greetings

Choosing how to greet a person for the first time can be a mess. One thing's for sure, never go in for a handshake; too corporate, too clammy.

The Room on the Third Floor

"We'd been chatting online for a few weeks. The day we were meant to go on our first date I got in a car accident on the way to the restaurant and broke my collar bone. She visited me in hospital every evening for a month. She'd bring snacks and we'd watch movies in my hospital bed. Five years later we're married with two kids. I guess we technically never had our first date."

Booooo oooooo ooo oo!

Ghosting someone leaves them with confusion and unanswered questions. It can cause a lot of pain. It might also really impact their view on dating again in the future, and that's not fair. The least you can do is be honest with the person you've been talking to; don't be so cowardly. If we could all run away from our problems we'd all be professional athletes.

People Who Like People

Whoever you're into, who gives a shit. Just be a nice person and treat other people well.

- Boys who like boys
- Boys who like manly boys
- Boys who like boys with beards
- Boys who like clean-shaven boys
- Boys who like girly boys
- Boys who like girls
- Boys who like boyish girls
- Boys who like girly girls
- Boys who like girls with tattoos
- Girls who like boys
- Girls who like bad boys*
- Girls who like nice boys
- Girls who like girls
- Girls who like girly girls
- Girls who like boyish girls
- Boys who like girls who like girls
- Boys who like girls and boys
- Girls who once liked boys but now like girls
- Boys who once liked girls but now like boys

*why?!

It's Giving Golden Retriever

You might find "bad boys" attractive, but wouldn't you rather be in a relationship with someone trustworthy and compassionate who you can proudly introduce to your mum, and know that when you sleep next to them at night, you're in safe hands? Give the good guys a chance. Ironically, they're the ones that get a bad rep.

Am I Interrupting?

"I once went on a date and they flirted with our waitress the entire time, making sure to tell her half-way through that we weren't together."

"No Offence, but..."

Insulting your date is not flirting, and it's not "banter". Whether it's commenting on what they're wearing, the food they've ordered or imitating their accent, what you find funny might be offensive to another person. There's teasing someone, and then there's being plain mean.

is for Vulnerability

Vulnerability means letting your guard down and allowing a person in without fear of rejection or criticism. It leads to genuine, wholesome, positive relationships with depth and substance. There's strength in vulnerability. Without it, the other person won't truly understand or know your wants and needs. This might sound scary, but you owe it to yourself. It'll lead to better communication, deeper connections and longer-lasting, authentic bonds.

A List of Sexy Things

1. Wiping your mouth
2. Not licking your knife
3. Being nice to animals
4. Letting them order first
5. Not interrupting the other person mid-sentence
6. Showing interest in the other person
7. Caring about the planet
8. Silently eating soup
9. Speaking nicely about your mum
10. Pouring their water first
11. Pleases, thank-yous and you're welcomes
12. Offering to split the bill
13. Covering your sneezes

Please Don't Call the Loo the "Little Boys' Room"

There are so many reasons why.

On that note, also refrain from referring to women as "birds", "hun", "love", "sweetheart" or "doll". Of course, context really matters, and it might come from an innocent place. But for the most part, these endearing terms come across as condescending. Get us on the wrong day and we just might get aggressive with it. Being told on a weekly basis to "Cheer up, love" by sweaty builders mid-scaffold is enough to bring on a karate chop as it is.

Be My Guest?

For anyone expecting a lady to spend the night, I'd suggest stocking up on the following:

- Tampons and pads
- Make-up wipes or remover
- Cotton pads

And in general, make sure you have:

- Toilet roll
- Shower gel
- Handwash
- A spare toothbrush and clean towel

If you want to be extra considerate and accommodating, stock up on coffee, milk and bread for the morning after.

A Complete and Utter Dumpster Fire

Unless your first date was a total shambles, a second one is always worth a shot. Don't expect butterflies or a 'spark' from the get-go. Loud, in-your-face people sometimes need a chance to simmer down and take their bravado mask off as much as a shy, reserved person might need time to warm up and come out of their shell. It's only fair to give it another go; things might be different the second time around.

Don't Get Your

Panties in a Pickle

It's OK if they don't text you back immediately; it doesn't mean they're not interested. Maybe you always have your phone within reaching distance, but it's not the same for everyone. People are busy. Maybe they don't check their phone at work because they find it distracting or they don't have the time to engage in back-and-forth chitchat. There could be many reasons for their lack of messaging. However, if it's taking three to five working days to get a response, that's a different story.

Seasonal Fling or Long-term Thing?

Are you after a bit of no-strings-attached fun, or something more meaningful? Know what you're looking for and be honest with the person. If your expectations don't match, then you could end up in a sticky situationship and hearts might get broken.

Stop Playing Mind Games

If you like them, tell them. If you want to text them, do it. There are no rules and playing it cool is really bad, ancient advice that'll most likely push the person away. Mystery isn't always attractive. If your flirting tactic is to keep your cards close to your chest, you might completely put them off you.

Being Fashionably Late Isn't a Thing

Rocking up twenty minutes late to a date gives off the wrong message. Don't intentionally keep them waiting; their time is just as valuable as yours. Being perfectly punctual is very Spring/Summer 2025.

P.S. If you're having doubts, don't cancel on the day. Give them at least 24 hours' notice or enough time to make other plans.

Drinks
DON'T
Have
Genders

A genuine overheard exchange:

M: I'll have a strawberry mojito.
W: Isn't that a bit girly?

If you consider some berries and rum "feminine" then you have some re-evaluating to do. Actually, the manliest of men like tiny pink umbrellas in their cocktails and cross their legs while sipping matcha lattes. Also, sophisticated ladies are partial to a nice cold pint of beer too, you know.

Fuckboys and Mean Girls

It's a romantic idea that you're capable of "fixing" or changing someone, but do you possess magical powers? As soon as you realize they're a fuckboy or mean girl, you should exit stage left. Don't hang around and don't be enticed back in. Too many of us have thought we'd be the one to change someone, but we never will. Trust somebody's actions, not what they say. Fuckboys might be charming and mean girls might be alluring, but since when did you have "mug" written on your forehead? Take the red pill, move on.

Sleeping on the Job

I've heard far too many horror stories about people who have started relationships at work. They're not all bad, but do you really want to be in a two-hour Zoom call with someone you once slept with on a drunken work night out? The same goes for breakups in-office; they're more unbearable than the job itself, I imagine.

Naked Umbrella Guy

"We'd been on a first date and it was pouring outside. He had an umbrella, so offered to walk me home. We got to my front door, and I told him a quick "thanks for tonight" and turned my back to leave. He started bawling his eyes out, muttering things through his tears like, "It's happened again" and "Nice guys always finish last". It was very odd and uncomfortable. I couldn't leave him like that on my doorstep in the pouring rain so I invited him in and went to get him a glass of water.

When I returned, he wasn't there anymore. I noticed my bedroom light had been turned on and the door was ajar. I walked into my room to find him standing there, naked, with his trousers in a puddle by his ankles. He stood there pink and panting. I threatened to call the police, called him every name under the sun and told him to get the fuck out. He slowly, sadly pulled his pants up and I marched him outside by his arm. Three months later he texted me saying he'd been reminiscing about the "amazing" night we'd had."

If You Wannabe My Lover

If you're unsure about someone, introduce them to your friends. Let them be the judge. Throw them to the wolves, I say! You might think they're right for you, but what's the opinion of your (brutally honest) Trustee Committee?

Step Up

Take what you learnt from your last relationship (if you have one) and apply it to the next one. Use this as an opportunity for self-reflection and re-evaluation. There's no such thing as a failed relationship, they're all life lessons. Sometimes they teach us how to be better people; whether it's how you could communicate better, trust deeper or be more vulnerable. Maybe it's recognizing what you thought you wanted in a person, versus what you actually need in a partner.

Instead of focusing on finding your perfect match, why not reframe it as looking for the person least wrong for you.

It's Not All About You

Conversations should be like a tennis match, so remember to ask questions. They're trying to get to know you and you should do the same. "How about you?", "What do you think?" Return their question and show the interest is mutual. Pick a detail from their story and follow up with an anecdote.

E.g. Them: This one time I was in Paris and a pigeon shat on my head.

You: Same! I was sitting on a park bench once when this happened to me. It's meant to be good luck!

Eager Beaver

It's easy to get overly excited about the person you're newly dating. Try not to plan the wedding on the second date. Having such high expectations so early on often leads to disappointment. It can also be intimidating (and dare I say, scary) for the other person if they know you're already researching honeymoon destinations.

Kisses and Concussions

"We were in the kitchen when he lent in to give me a kiss that I wasn't wanting or expecting. I think I screamed, "No, thank you!" and turned around so quickly and with such force that I fell over the bin and hit my head on the counter. We sat in silence for the next hour while he held a pack of frozen peas to my forehead."

It's **NOT** Like the Movies

Relationships are hard work. Life events, financial pressures and external factors are all things that can rock the boat occasionally. It's your job as a united force to protect your bubble from harm and to support each other when things get tough.

A recipe for a healthy partnership includes:

- A foundation of friendship
- A dollop of communication
- Intimacy, both emotionally and physically
- Active listening
- Oodles of laughter
- Heaps of trust
- A healthy sprinkling of disagreements and heated debates

Coffee First, Food Later

Dinner on the first date is pretty hardcore. Trying to seductively shovel a juicy burger into your mouth while attempting to maintain eye contact isn't for the faint-hearted. Drinks first can always lead to a spontaneous dinner afterwards. Keep your options open so that if you're not feeling it, you're not committed to anything more. A coffee or a dog walk makes it easier to wrap things up quickly and bid them farewell.

What Language Are You Speaking?

The way we receive and express love can be categorized into five love languages. It can be helpful to know what yours is. They are:

- **Words of affirmation:** Telling your partner they are the sexiest/cleverest/kindest thing you've ever encountered.

- **Quality time:** Hanging out and doing fun stuff just the two of you.

- **Physical touch:** An arm around them while watching TV, a hand on their knee in the car.

- **Acts of service:** Doing their laundry, making them their favourite meal.

- **Receiving gifts:** It doesn't matter what it is or what it cost; little gestures show you care.

Personally, I enjoy having my hair stroked as I'm being told how fabulous I am, while waiting for my homecooked meal to be served. Is that too much to ask?

To Birria,

Or Not to Birria?

Eat on your date. Don't be the person that orders the salad when you really want the bolognese/ribs/chicken wings/tacos. The least you can do is enjoy the meal. Just maybe avoid adventurous cuisines at first. You never know what intolerances or bowel issues people have these days.

Air Your Laundry

If you have a kid, hate your job or are going through a divorce, be open about it. Honesty is always appreciated. Having said that...

... maybe don't talk about your ex on the first date.

Arrogant Assumptions

'This girl knew I was a veggie but insisted we go to a burger place. She then made me pay. This was the same girl that asked to come back to mine and when I said no, she said it was extremely arrogant of me to assume she wanted to sleep with me.'

Red, Orange and Yellow Flags

Identify your own non-negotiables before
running for the hills.

Hates cats
Mean: red flag

Lives with six cats
Concerning: also a red flag

Enjoys a game of Scrabble
Wholesome: green flag

Gets aggressive playing board games
Disturbing: red flag

Partial to chicken nuggets
Nice: green flag

Will only eat chicken nuggets
Troublesome: major red flag

Don't Be
Gross

**Sexual innuendos are really naff
and off-putting.**

**Wet sauces and moist cheesecakes.
We've heard it all before.
Have some class, darling.**

A Conversation Over a Dating App

Hey, how are you?

4 hours later

Hey! Good thanks, you?

24 hours later

What you up to today?

2 hours later

Just at work.
What about you?

*Continues for the rest of time *

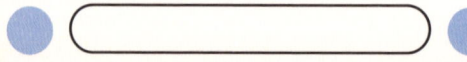

Arriving Alone vs. Waiting Alone

You have a choice of either walking into the restaurant alone when you know they're already sitting at the table (so cringey when you're trying to spot their face that you might've only seen in a photo on an app taken five years ago among a sea of people), or arriving first and having to do the awkward wait alone. I'm guessing you'll either be clutching your phone, staring at the clock or studying the menu. A quick game of Tetris to make you look busy can't hurt.

Whatever you do, please don't be scrolling through a dating app or replying to any new DMs.

Don't Be Creepy

Doing a deep dive on their Instagram before the first date means you might let it slip that you know exactly where they went on holiday six years ago, what they wore, what they ate and who they were dating. And God forbid you accidentally 'like' the post. It's a dangerous rabbit hole and I don't trust your acting skills.

By all means, let your friends do a LinkedIn background check; it's the safest way to remain incognito.

Liar, Liar, Pants on Fire!

Don't portray a false version of yourself. That'd be you lying to them, as well as yourself. Not only that, but pretending to be the person you think they want is very presumptuous.

Your dating profile must be accurate. I once matched with someone online and thanks to their photos they looked extremely tall. When I met them, my jaw dropped. They barely came up to my elbow. I spent the rest of the evening very distracted. Quite frankly, I could think of nothing else and it took everything within me to resist saying something. Don't waste your own time or others' by posting deceiving representations of yourself.

The Escape Route

Hatch a plan for when you need to end the date quickly.
Here are some get outs:

"I should make a move, I've...

... got an early start tomorrow.

... got to help my flatmate with...

... got a call with someone in [insert country
with significant time difference].

... got to stop by my mum's on the way home."

"Hey Girl!"

When you start chatting to your own reflection(s) in the mirror, singing to yourself on the toilet or complimenting everyone in line by the hand dryers, that's when you might be a little too merry, and should go home, safely. If it's late or dark and you're at all concerned, share your live location with a friend.

Along Came Poly

Open relationships are becoming more and more of a thing. They can definitely work, but only with a strong foundation of honesty and openness, as well as setting some clear boundaries to make sure everyone involved feels safe and happy in this new dynamic. It's important that this is something you both want and not an excuse for one of you to misbehave. It would be wrong to feel like this is the last resort to "save" your relationship or to feel pressured into doing it for fear of losing your partner.

- Is this someone you're both welcoming into the relationship?
- Or is this someone you're both dating separately?
- Will your partner meet them?
- What are the rules on safe sex?
- Is this person a specific gender?
- What are the rules on meeting your friends and family?
- Will you be bringing this person home?
- Will they be sleeping over?
- Will you share details of your sexual escapades with your partner?

Make sure you establish these boundaries before embarking on an open relationship. You might find things can get messy without them.

The Scientific Stuff

These chemical messengers, along with oxytocin, are rapidly released in our brain when we lock eyes with someone we find attractive. The combination makes us giddy and euphoric and causes a reduction in serotonin, which can lead to loss of appetite and insomnia – similar to the aftermath of a bad breakup. It's true that you can be so infatuated with someone that you can't eat or sleep.

On top of that, brain scans of people in love have shown that the "reward" centres of the brain fire up when people are shown a photo of someone they are intensely attracted to. So, even if you wanted to play it cool, all this crazy behaviour isn't in your control. You can blame evolution for that.

This is dopamine.

This is norepinephrine.

Oh Baby, Baby.
How Was I Supposed to Know?

There's nothing wrong with messaging them the next day saying you weren't into the date. It's the right thing to do. Don't use a lame excuse; show the person some respect and be truthful and upfront about your reasoning. They'll appreciate it.

Don't Let Anyone Mistreat You, Ever

If they do or say anything that makes you feel uncomfortable or unsafe, leave.

You don't owe them anything.

The Toothpick Twiddler

"He was twiddling a toothpick in between his teeth. Probably to try and look sexy. Someone knocked his chair from behind and the toothpick went straight through the roof of his mouth. The date ended in A&E."

Not My Typo

Make your dating bio as strong as it can be. Check for typos; know your "there" from your "their", and your "you're" from your "your". Everyone seems to mention loving the same three things: food, music and travelling. Come on, you can do better than that. Include something unique to you that will spark a conversation or question. Get creative with it.

Are They an Actual Real-life Person?

Catfishing is still alive and well. Sadly, that MTV show didn't discourage everyone.

It's wise to FaceTime before your date. If they refuse or give an odd reason, that's a ginormous red flag and I'd stay at home if I were you.

O is for Oysters

An exotic bird drops dead from the sky every time someone spots oysters on a menu and exclaims,

"YOU BETTER WATCH OUT! DID YOU KNOW THEY'RE AN APHRODISIAC?"

Where the Magic Happens

For the love of Cupid, do not under any circumstances point at your bed and declare, "This is where the magic happens."

What magic? Do you conduct spells in your bedroom? Do you store a cauldron under your bed? Do you muster up potions in your spare time? Will your guest transform into a frog at the stroke of midnight?

Unless there's a wand in your wardrobe and an owl in your cupboard, there's absolutely no magic present. If anything, the deed will be done in a matter of minutes, your mattress is stained, your sheets are musty and your saggy pillows haven't been replaced in years.

Sexy Triangles

Non-verbal cues are important, specifically good eye
contact. To do the sexy eyeball method you need
to be in an intimate setting, sitting across the
table from your date. While listening to them
talk, glance at their left eye for one second,
then briefly down at their lips for two
seconds and then back up to their
right eye. It's meant to enhance
a deeper connection and
is apparently the
ultimate flirting
magic
trick

.

Take Your Phone off the Table

On your date, don't be distracted by the group chat blowing up or your notifications. Filming every dish as it lands on your table can also be really off-putting. You're there to be actively present with the other person, so social media can wait. It's just good manners. Put your phone in your bag or in a different room. Even having it lying on the table face down can be distracting. It's almost like you're saying, "You've got my attention, but not all of it."

A Fine Line

Don't confuse these things with confidence:

- Keeping your sunglasses on indoors
- Bragging about how much money you make
- Overly commenting on how attractive you are
- Boasting about your Iron Man PB
- Sharing how many dates you've been on or how many people you've slept with recently

Personally, I find nothing uglier than a person repeatedly commenting on how attractive they are. Immediately, no.

Be Honest About Your Weird Stuff

If you've got quirky hobbies, share them. Who knows?
Maybe they're also partial to a bit of soap carving.
There's no point trying to hide these things; it'll come
out eventually, ya lil' weirdo.

A Lesson Learnt

"I realised towards the end of my relationship that they never wanted to hang out with my friends. All our weekend plans revolved around them seeing their people. When we broke up I found myself having to apologise to all the friends I hadn't seen in ages; I had a lot of making-up to do. It was only then that I realised how isolated I'd been and how one-sided the relationship was. They didn't want to involve themselves in my life or make an effort with the people who mattered to me. It's something I'll know to look out for in the future."

Taking the Initiative Is Sensual, Seductive and Saucy

Being told a time and place to be is very attractive, IMHO. Sometimes it's nice not to do any of the thinking; just make sure you return the favour.

Play the Field, but Not Too Much

Having numerous sexual partners isn't a bad thing, as long as it makes you happy. Just be sure to get regular STI checks, use protection and don't hurt people along the way.

Make an Effort to Feel Good About Yourself

Walk with confidence, act with grace and speak positively about yourself. My grandma used to look in the mirror and tell her reflection, "This is as good as it's gonna get today," and I can't help but think this is a great thing to put into practice.

You Is Kind
You Is Smart
You Is Impor'ant

Compliments are cool, so dish them out. Also, don't say negative things about your personality or appearance. And don't even think about rejecting compliments. If they tell you you're pretty, say thank you. If they call you clever, say thank you. Don't do yourself dirty.

 1-800-BABY-CAKES

You know it's heading somewhere when you change
their name in your phone.

My love ♥♥♥♥

Lover

Loverboy

My world ;-)

My everything

My Lady

Queen

My King

Handsome

Babbbbyyyyyyyyy ♥

Babyface

Beautiful

Bubzie

Bubz :-)

Bubsy Malone

Baebeeeee ✿

Bae

B.

Self-worth, Baby

Know your value and acknowledge when someone's not stepping up to the mark. You are deserving of someone who recognises your worth, respects you, values your presence, and supports you wholeheartedly. Walking away from a situationship that no longer serves you is better for your self-worth in the long run. Invest time, effort and energy into yourself and things that make you happy, rather than someone that leaves you confused and doubting yourself.

You won't be lucky in love if you haven't learnt to love yourself first. It's important to find someone who compliments and nourishes your life, not someone who merely exists because you're bored or the bed feels empty.

It's Possible to Fall in Love Several Times

It might have happened to you once before, and it can happen again. You can have numerous loves of your life.

That past relationship didn't work out and you might have loved them with your entire being but here's the thing; that was then, and this is now. Your heart doesn't have limitations, and the amount of love you have to give and will receive doesn't expire. Don't go into dating with the idea that you found love once, and that was your only shot at happiness.

Bills and Butter

Relationships require patience, compassion and compromise. It's not all Sundays spent in bed, handwritten notes and sunset walks on the beach. In all honesty, a healthy relationship is relatively boring for the most part; it's two people trying to get through life's troubles without losing their minds or love for one another.

Some realistic relationship scenarios include:

- Fighting over who's going to take the bins out
- Fighting over the fact you forgot to take the bins out
- Going to sleep without saying goodnight
- Mundane discussions about what's for dinner
- Mundane discussions about buying butter, milk or bin liners
- Boring chats about the car needing petrol or the boiler needing servicing
- Arguments over taking the dog to the vet
- Job worries, health worries, family worries, mortgage worries and childcare worries
- All the other worries

Everyone knows no "happy" couple actually cuddles before falling asleep. They mumble goodnight, roll over and silently scroll on their phones until their fingers are numb and they can't see clearly anymore.

Stop Comparing Them to Your Ex

They might not have the same interests or sense of humour. Maybe you don't have the same discussions or "inside" jokes. That's because they're different people and they shouldn't be compared. They're your ex for a reason; isn't it a good thing they're not a carbon copy? Stop being in your head about it.

Don't Forget Your Friends

Always make time for your buddies when you're in a relationship. It can be tricky, but try not to spend every waking minute with your partner because if worse comes to worst and the two of you don't survive the test of time, it can be very difficult to crawl back into your friends' lives if you have spent the past year neglecting them.

As much as binge-watching Netflix on the sofa and eating takeaway every weekend appeals to the majority of us, you must get out and do separate stuff with your friends. It's important.

Chemistry Is Not Compatibility

You start talking, go on a date and begin hanging out. You believe you've met your person, that the stars have aligned and that it's meant to be. Or is it? Is it real chemistry, or is it your pattern? Do they seem perfect because they remind you of your toxic ex, who also seemed perfect in the beginning? Do you feel at home because you're used to being mistreated? Does it feel like fate because they remind you of that one person who it never worked out with? It's easy to slip into old habits when it comes to our love lives because they are what we've become accustomed to. Like most things that aren't good for us, it's hard to break free from unhealthy cycles. If you're frank and honest with yourself, you'll learn to make the necessary changes, both for your mental and emotional well-being.

Don't Mistake
Turbulence
for Passion

Toxicity is addictive; don't confuse a toxic relationship with a "passionate" one. On one day, and off the next. You know it's not right, but you keep getting sucked back in. It's called trauma bonding. There's a certain thrill or excitement wrapped up in unhealthy relationships because you never know where you stand, and it keeps things "interesting". But it's not. It's not normal to cry over someone more than you laugh with them. It's not normal to lie awake at night paranoid or worried. To fear the phone call or text messages, or not to receive any at all. Toxic relationships are difficult to get out of and can take a long time to heal from. Watch out for the signs and put yourself, your safety and your well-being first.

"There's Plenty More Fish"

is a fucking stupid phrase. And also...

Global Warming Is KILLING All the Fish

Things You Should Know About Life

Advice is bias.

The other sock will go missing.

If you can't afford to buy it three times,
don't buy it at all.

Hairdressers will lie to you.

You'll kill some plants.

You'll shrink your linen trousers.

It's impossible to cook the correct
amount of pasta.

You'll overpluck something.

Family fallouts happen at funerals.

Everyone has days when everything seems shit.

Don't dive into swimming pools headfirst.

Always take your make-up off.

Wipe from front to back.

You'll lose faith sometimes in boys,
in friends, in yourself.

Your heart will get broken.

You'll break someone's heart.

Speaking of broken hearts, turn the page for breakups
and heart aches...

Congrats on Your Breakup!

The other side of dating is when it all goes downhill and you land in broken hearted territory. Have faith, it's always better to be out of a relationship than in the wrong one. And you did it! You broke free of the situation. The genie has left the lamp!

It's time to invest in yourself and get excited for what or who lies ahead. Sometimes it's a reason to celebrate.

A new beginning is in store (and probably a new haircut).

Sayonara!

Auf Wiedersehen!

Adios!

Ciao!

The Event

Whether you've initiated the breakup or someone has broken up with you, all breakups suck. It's never nice when a relationship ends. Breaking up with someone involves all kinds of emotions — including guilt and worry — as well as wanting to support and check in on the other person (but not too much for fear of crossing boundaries). The person on the receiving end of the breakup often experiences shock or feelings of rejection and despair. Often, we might not have a good enough reason, just a feeling that something's not quite right.

What went wrong? Am I not enough? Should we give it another go?

Even when it's a mutual decision it can be a very confusing time filled with disappointment and hurt. One thing's for sure though: you won't be the same person you were before the breakup. They're transformative things.

Try not to think of it as time that's been wasted. Be kind to yourself and give yourself the space and time to process things. It's like grief in that sense, so treat it that way.

Your Brain Is Teasing You

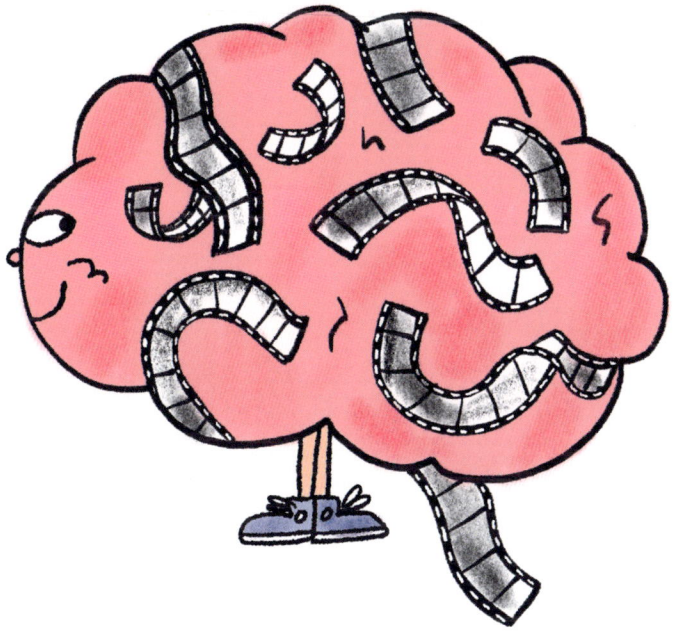

The romcom montage playing in your mind of happy times is a distorted version of events. There's a saying that goes: "Don't trust how you feel now, just what you knew then". There's a scientific reason why your brain commits such foolery, but I haven't done the research, so feel free to do so and take off the rose-tinted glasses.

Achy Breaky

Why does it hurt so bad? Remember our chemical friends oxytocin, dopamine and serotonin? Well, too much of a good thing can be bad. When we experience heartbreak, these levels drop, while stress hormones such as cortisol, adrenaline, and noradrenaline increase. These "heartbreak hormones" can cause physical symptoms such as pain.

You're not being dramatic; after a breakup the anterior cingulate cortex can overstimulate the vagus nerve, causing chest pain, nausea or muscle tightness. You're not wrong if you've felt as though you're having heart palpitations or your chest feels heavy.

In a nutshell, love can be the best and the worst. It can be the thing that gets you up in the morning, but it can equally be the reason you can't get out of bed at all.

Things That Break Easily

- The porcelain plate your mum's had since the 70s
- The giant mirror in your bedroom
- A Fabergé egg
- An antique vase
- Trust

Miley Cyrus said nothing breaks like a heart, and I can confirm.

Life Is Great. Everything Sucks!

I hate them.

I miss them.

I feel awesome!

Everything sucks.

They were the best.

I hate them with a firing passion.

Life is good!

I miss them.

What a piece of shit.

My heart hurts.

We were good together, weren't we?

I am depressed.

I'm going to be single forever.

Single and ready to mingle!

Will I ever feel normal again?

I hope they burn in hell.

To hell with them.

I curse the day they were born.

I hate them with the power of a thousand suns.

Bad News

It's going to hurt when you find out they're in a new relationship. You'll be angry, then sad, then you'll be intrigued. Don't let it get the better of you; no good will come of hunting down their new partner on social media. You'll find yourself comparing things, picturing things, imagining things, regretting things and questioning things, and it's not worth putting yourself through that. It's better to remain blissfully ignorant.

last seen today at 2:56am

Why aren't they responding to your essay? Who are they with? Where are they? Have they even read it?

The online status, read receipts and the "last seen" features are the worst things about WhatsApp. Turn them off if you can bear it, or you'll end up getting square eyes staring at your phone for hours on end. There are better ways to spend your time. Don't torment yourself.

From Lovers to Strangers

The grieving. The adjustment. The sheer weirdness of it. You once knew all the ins and outs about this person. All their dreams and secrets. All their intricacies and quirks. Everything that made them unique. Now you don't even know what country they live in.

You invest months or years into learning and appreciating everything about them for it all to fizzle out and end one day. Often, you're not sure where it began to go wrong. It gets easier and more comfortable to live with as time goes on.

wallow

But not for too long. It's acceptable to spend days in bed feeling sorry for yourself surrounded by tears, tissues and cookie crumbs, but there comes a point when you must shower, get out of the house, breathe some fresh air and seize the damn day.

A List of All the Things That Annoyed You About Them

I'll start:

- The way they never put the cap back on the toothpaste
- The way they loaded the dishwasher
- The way they chewed all the pens
- The way they could never decide what to have for dinner
- The way their teeth scraped the fork every time they took a bite
- The way they never replaced the loo roll
- The way they pronounced "chipotle"
- The way they'd leave their underwear on the bathroom floor

Your turn.

It's Not Just Your Song

That really rare, obscure song that you both consider to be specifically yours because it comes on at weird times in unexpected places and the lyrics reflect your own love story, most definitely doesn't just belong to the two of you. At first, you'll feel a mini punch to the gut every time the first three chords play. Then, one day it'll come on the radio and you won't even notice. Or you will, and you'll simply acknowledge it and smile.

So, to clarify, that time you were horseback riding in the middle of the Cuban mountains when out of nowhere you could hear the Lighthouse Family faintly in the distance — no, that wasn't a sign. The universe has better things to do.

The C-Word

Make sure you get closure. It's really important if you're needing clarity and have unanswered questions or things left to say.

The same goes the other way too; make sure you give them the closure they need. Just know that you might never get the answers you want, and sometimes you just won't ever understand.

The Other C-Word

There are many different interpretations on what is considered "cheating". It can be emotional as well as physical. It's murky waters, especially if you are not in a monogamous relationship, but if they have:

- Been regularly messaging someone behind your back
- Been intimate or kissed someone else
- Flirted with people when you're not around
- Engaged in conversation online/in person with someone with a flirtatious or sexual undertone
- Exchanged numbers with someone with the wrong intention
- Still have a profile on a dating app

Then you can be sure they've got a hidden agenda. Stop questioning yourself or justifying their actions; it's 100% cheating and you deserve better.

If you are guilty of any of the opposite, it's sneaky and hurtful and no matter the reasoning, it's selfish. You need to question why you did it and why you're in a relationship in the first place. Investing trust in someone after being cheated on and lied to is very challenging and requires a lot of work on both sides. It's not easy coming back from betrayal.

Just know, if they've been unfaithful, it doesn't necessarily mean they don't love or care for you. It could be for a number of reasons, such as low self-esteem or feeling emotionally neglected in your relationship. This isn't me making allowances. Like I said, it's murky waters.

Heartbreak Hotel

If you meet up with them post-breakup, just know you might end up in their bed. Have a good think about what your boundaries are before meeting up, when for whatever reason you may no longer be thinking rationally. Let's not complicate things further; do you want to have the cake and eat it too?

Sushi Sadness

"My ex broke up with me in a Japanese restaurant at the sushi counter. I haven't been able to have a salmon and avocado handroll since. That was four years ago."

Question Marks and Broken Hearts

It's normal to think about them, even years later. Truth be told, some people will haunt us for a lifetime. One of the worst parts of a breakup is not knowing if you're the one feeling most of the pain as they go about their lives.

Where are they now?

Did they change the colour of their hair?

Are they with anyone?

Do they miss you?

Where do they work?

Did they get any more tattoos?

Did they move?

Do they even live in the same country?

What do they do now?

Did they ever fix the leak in the ceiling?

How is their mum?

Did they get a dog?

Did they learn to drive?

Did they start that business?

Do they still have trouble sleeping?

Does that song remind them of you too?

Do their friends mention you?

Do they ever cry about you?

Have they gone back to any of those places again?

Do they do all those things with someone else now?

Do they regret how it ended?

Are you their favourite?

Do they ever think about calling you?

Do they ever play back your voice notes?

Do they ever read your old texts?

Process

shit

First, it'll be really shit, then it'll get less shit.
Then one day, you'll have forgotten the shit.

Initiating Self-DESTRUCT Mode

Buying plants and pets.

New piercings in weird places.

Regrettable tattoos.

Dying your hair crazy colours (sometimes shaving it off altogether).

Losing your phone, your wallet and your inhibitions.

Partying too much, not drinking enough water.

Coming home at odd hours.

Waking up in strangers' beds.

Too much kebab, not enough kale.

Lots of crazy, not enough calm.

Things That Suck the Most

When you've watched a film, heard a song or seen a meme that you know they'd love, but you're not talking to each other. All you want to do is chat about it with them and you can't. It's borderline torture. Consider having a friend on standby who can be your soundboard instead. Yes, it's not the same, but it's something.

Tissues on Transport

Modes of transportation might make you cry. Sometimes it's because of a cute elderly couple, and sometimes it's a brand-new baby. Other times, it's a wave of sadness that'll slap you in the face when you're sitting on the bus.

Feel the Feels

There are seven stages of grieving a breakup. It can be different for everyone, and you might experience all, none or some of these. It can be helpful to understand where you're at and know that you're not alone.

1. **WHY:** You might be in disbelief at the situation and not understand how you've arrived here.

2. **DENIAL:** Believing that this isn't the end and you can fix things.

3. **BARGAINING:** Willing to do anything to avoid accepting it's over.

4. **RELAPSE:** Potentially convincing the other person that it's worth another try.

5. **HATE AND ANGER:** Feeling overwhelming negative emotions towards the situation and the other person.

6. **SURRENDERING:** Accepting the fact it's over and hopefully understanding the reasons why.

7. **LOOKING FORWARDS:** Feeling hopeful that this is for the best and better things lie ahead.

Breakups have the power to bring out the worst in us, making us act in ways we never knew we could, or struggle to understand. It can be shocking and scary not to recognise these parts of us. Trust me, I've questioned my sanity before.

Ex Marks the Spot

"'My ex found out I'd cheated on her. She left me a lovely surprise the following morning when I discovered a human shit on my car's bonnet. The neighbours captured her doing the deed on their security camera."

Keep It Classy

Don't go running your mouth, in person or on social media. You never know what's going to get back to them through your sister's friend's once-removed cousin's best friend's colleague at a wedding. Juicy gossip travels fast and you don't want to give them a reason to think badly of you. Don't you want to appear like you've handled this with grace and decorum? Bitching is tacky, baby girl.

Light Switches

It's on, then it's off. One minute you're giving each other space, then you're giving it another go, then it slowly starts to fall apart again. Uncertainty is the bitch of breakups. It's all very stressful and tiring. If you're losing sleep, friendships or other aspects of your life are suffering, there comes a point when you're going to have to make an executive decision and call it quits. Or stick with it, and over time you'll run out of fucks to give.

Let Yourself Miss Them

There's beauty in reminiscing on the good times and the moments you shared. It can feel quite cathartic.

Years from now, when your heart has healed and you no longer have a bitter taste in your mouth, you might think of the person with fondness. Maybe you'll find yourself thanking them for what they taught you about love, relationships and yourself.

Their Mum

A breakup can sometimes mean letting go of the relatives you formed meaningful relationships with. It can be really tough, especially if you started to consider them family. You probably shared significant events together, like Christmas days and birthday dinners. Unfortunately, one of the trade-offs we make when we enter into relationships is the lovely people we may lose along the way.

Oh, the Places You'll Cry!

Bath/shower/sea. Sometimes you'll stare out the window of a moving vehicle listening to sad songs and reminiscing, by choice.

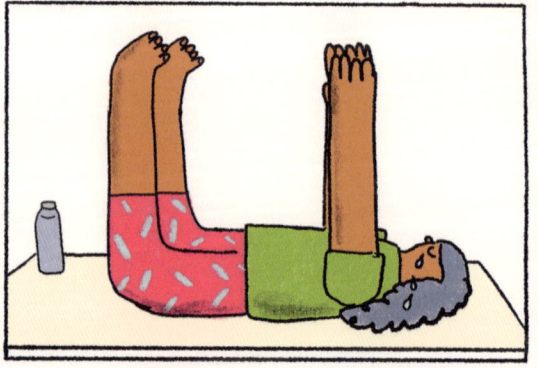

Trust Your Tummy

Your vagus nerve carries signals between your brain, heart and digestive system. That sinking feeling in your gut or that dull chest pain you've experienced is nature's way of telling you something is not quite right. There really is truth in having a hunch about someone or something; you should trust that feeling of discomfort when it comes to all matters of love.

Suspicious Minds

"I swore I'd never go through their phone but after months of her taking it to the shower with her and sleeping with it under her pillow I finally cracked. Turns out, I was right all along and she'd been cheating on me for months with an "old friend". We broke up. To this day she denies it even though I've read all the texts. I've had trust issues in every relationship since."

Don't Listen to Sad Music/ Watch Sad Films on Aeroplanes*

*The altitude makes you cry more

Survivin' and Thrivin'

Embrace the singleness. The bed is now yours.
Not sharing your food is great. Those long good-morning
texts and goodnight messages were annoying anyway.
Now there's more money in your account and more
time to spend with friends. Also, you can grow your
leg hair and flirting is back on the menu, enjoy!

Get Physical

There are countless benefits to exercising for your mental health. Just half an hour of exercise two to three times a week will boost your mood and positivity. Get outside, breathe in some fresh air and get those steps up. Do it while on the phone to a friend or sipping on some coffee. Not only will it help clear your head, but you'll physically feel better. If you choose swimming, no one will see your tears.

Don't Force It

Wait until you're definitely ready before joining any dating apps. It's important you're in the right state of mind, so you should not start dating again until you're feeling like you've processed the past. Without realising, you might be doing it as a way of seeking validation but that'll only result in a bruised ego or a battered self-esteem. With dating comes the risk of rejection and it might knock you ten steps backwards, leaving you feeling even more helpless and confused. Heal first.

And remember: hurt people hurt people.

Cups of Cocoa

Surround yourself with old friends and the people who know you best. Good friends pick you up when you're down, fill you with kind words and positive affirmations and are willing to listen. They know you well and want the best for you, and that's what you need right now. Friends are like a warm cup of cocoa on a winter's day. Doesn't that sound cozy and comforting?

God Forbid a Stranger Walks Past You With Their Smell On

Avoid perfume departments in shopping centres. Avoid the duty-free shops at the airport. Consider going about your day wearing those nose plugs swimmers use.

Stop the Pity Party

It was only ever you.

You were meant for me.

You complete me.

If I let you go, maybe you'll come back.

You're the love of my life.

I'm nothing without you.

I'll never find someone like you.

Right person, wrong time.

Maybe in the next lifetime.

Again, it's the movies talking.

Be. The.
BIGGER.
Person.

It might feel like you're letting yourself down or doing yourself an injustice, but often, it's better to make peace with a situation than to harbour negative feelings or resentment towards a person. It's not weak, it's protecting your hurt and your heart. It's the grown thing to do.

Bob the Builder

Get fixing. Your trust might be broken, your pride might be shattered and your ego might be bruised, but now is an opportunity for you to work on other aspects of your life that'll help you build back your confidence. Rediscover old passions, learn a new skill or treat yourself to some well-deserved pampering. Use this time as an opportunity to meet new friends. You've got all the tools to start feeling yourself again.

Cryptic Captions

Avoid long social media threads and writing philosophical, cryptic captions on your posts. (Hint: they're never cryptic, it's not going to get their attention, it won't change the situation for the better and it's a little embarrassing.)

#healing #singleAF #newbeginnings #unbreakable #strongerthanever

Reply...

Wish You Were Here or Wish We Were There?

Because of reminders of better times with them, you might be putting off visiting certain places for the time being. Fear not; one day you'll feel like strolling along the Champs-Élysées or Khaosan Road once again. You might even do it with your new person. In the meantime, work on rewiring your brain. Make new memories in places once haunted by your ex. Go and see that band you both loved. Go to that restaurant, book that trip you talked about or visit that museum from your first date. Rewrite the memories in your head and make new ones.

Don't Send Durnk Txtsss xx

Your inebriated brain will tell you it's a good idea, but trust me on this: give your phone to a friend if you don't have the willpower to resist drunk-texting them. Or worse still, sending drunk voice notes. Next-morning you will hate previous-evening you. You'll be embarrassed and angry and oh-so-disappointed in yourself. And don't blame the cocktails; Aperols don't have thumbs.

Instead, might I suggest...

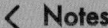 

21 October at 10:19

The Notes App

A very handy tool for drafting passive aggressive texts that should probably never be sent.

Sleep on it and revisit it the next day. Sometimes, saying nothing says it all.

Alternatively, use your phone to jot down your thoughts and feelings and save them to share with your therapist.

No
Excuses
No
Exceptions

You don't owe them anything. Protect your mind, your heart and your health, and walk away with your head held high. Better things (and partners) lie ahead.

Now and Then

Years will go by and you'll be washing the dishes or stuck in traffic and a wave of sadness will creep up on you. Maybe it's their birthday, or what would've been your anniversary. Maybe it was that bloody song on the radio or someone in the street you thought looked like them. You'll be there, frozen, missing them and thinking things like, "We could've made it work" or, "We had a great thing" or, "Why did we give up?" Maybe you'll question the reasons why it ended or you've forgotten altogether. You're thinking those things because time has passed and you've healed. You've dealt with it all. This is who you are now, not the person you were all that time ago. Don't question yourself. Have no regrets; leave it in the past and focus on your future.

Get Your Shit Together

Collect your stuff from their place as soon as you can, and take a friend if that helps. Arrange for your ex to leave the premises beforehand. Put some happy music on – something fast paced and instrumental like samba is a good choice.

Be extra certain you check:

- Under the bed
- In the bathroom cabinets
- The bedside tables
- Behind the sofa
- The actual walls
- The 'everything' kitchen drawer

And don't forget:

- That pair of odd earrings
- Those old trainers
- Your plants

Be sure to leave no trace behind. The idea is that you don't have a reason to return or get in touch again. For those extra traumatic breakups where you share many things and allocating them is hard, itemized spreadsheets can help.

Got a Text!

That feeling when your phone lights up and it's not them.
Or it is, and it's a brand new extra-long display of angry
words, explanations and accusations. Both scenarios are
equally full of dread.

Chuck your phone into the nearest body of water,
lock it away in a dark box and throw away the key,
blindfold yourself, or hide it some place you'll forget
to avoid all possible eventualities.

Boomerang

It's not always true that if you let something go, it'll come back to you.

You know what keeps coming back though? Herpes. So, be careful out there.

A Tequila Tray of Tears

"I'd just broken up with my long-term girlfriend. We were sitting at the dining table and she was crying. I was consoling her when my extremely drunk flatmate burst in holding a tray of shots telling us how perfect we were for each other and asking when we were getting married."

Avocado on Toast

I had a long-term relationship
end over half an avocado. It wasn't
the avocado itself, but that was the
cherry on top. The final thing. The straw
that broke the camel's back. I'm not saying
be wary of avocados, but I am saying
relationships can end in the weirdest,
most nonsensical of ways.

Hide the Evidence

Place all photos and memorabilia
out of sight. The padlock from Paris?
Your first cinema ticket? Their baggy
pyjama tee? Those passport photo
strips? Shove them in a cardboard
box. No one's saying don't keep
them, one fine day you might
appreciate the memories, but
right now they can fuck right off.

STOP
Stalking

Get off their socials. Remove them as friends. Block them if you have no willpower. It only leads to bad discoveries. On that note, consider getting off social media in general. Removing or deleting some apps for a bit might make all the difference to your mental health and clarity. Everyone's in need of a pause now and then; get into the real world and out of the one in your hand. Also, remember to delete your shared calendar – you don't need to know what day they've got the gym or a dentist appointment. Unhelpful.

The
Cold-hearted
Truth

They weren't
meant for you.
There are eight billion
people in the world.
Your person exists.

It's Not for You, Honey Boo

Been there, tried that, failed miserably. It's common to think "I still want you in my life" after splitting up but do you really believe that's a wise move? In reality you're prolonging the pain and the struggle to get over each other. Inevitably, one of you will meet someone new and it'll hurt all over again, like a fresh wound being ripped open. Unless it's absolutely unavoidable – you work together, you share a dog, or your best friends are married to each other – remove them from your life.

No one needs a shadow of their past lurking around. Shake hands, bid the relationship adieu and go your separate ways.

Say Sorry

Unless it was entirely their fault, in which case, they can fuck off, and let's pray karma gets them.

A Happy

Ending

Not everyone wants to date. Not everyone wants a partner. And not everyone is looking for love. Some people enjoy flying solo, and that's totally cool and valid. Whatever brings you joy, peace and happiness.

You don't need another "half" to be complete. If there's anything to take away from this book, it's to love, respect and value yourself. You're worth all the best things in life and that can be found in friendships, family, new experiences, seeing the world, good food and mostly any alcoholic beverage (unless you're teetotal, in which case, dessert?).

Thank You, Next

To my partner (or my better three-quarters): thank goodness I'll never have to go on a date again. You're great. 10/10.

An XL thank you to the brilliant team at Laurence King. Collaborating with you is always a pleasure, and you've brought this idea to life beautifully. Special thanks to Hannah Coughlin for her guidance and insight and for sharing the vision right from the start.

To Liam and Irina for the art and design work; I couldn't be prouder of this book. Big thanks and a gargantuan round of applause to the exceptionally talented Hannah Jacobs for the illustrations and for taking my silly notes seriously.

To Lily Wombles for her time and conversation. Endless gratitude to Holly Faulks, for having all the conversations I'd rather avoid. Last but not least, my third big thank you to the O.G; Elen Jones.

First published in Great Britain in 2025
by Laurence King, an imprint
of The Orion Publishing Group Ltd.,
Carmelite House, 50 Victoria Embankment,
London EC4Y 0DZ

the legal stuff!

An Hachette UK Company

The authorised representative in the EEA is Hachette Ireland,
8 Castlecourt Centre, Dublin 15, D15 XTP3, Ireland (email: info@hbgi.ie)

10 9 8 7 6 5 4 3 2 1

Text © 2025 Carina Maggar
Illustrations © 2025 Hannah Jacobs

A CIP catalogue record for this book is
available from the British Library.

ISBN (Paperback) 978 1 39962 767 2
ISBN (eBook) 978 1 39962 768 9

Commissioning Editor: Hannah Coughlin
Art Director: Liam Relph
Designer: Irina Selaru
Senior Production Controller: Sarah Cook

Origination by f1 colour Ltd

Printed in China by C&C Offset Printing Co. Ltd.

MIX
Paper | Supporting
responsible forestry
FSC® C104740

www.laurenceking.com
www.orionbooks.co.uk